Mind

Of

The Speechless

By

Myn'less Koncept

Mind of the Speechless

Copyright © 2020 by Diamond King aka Myn'less Koncept

All rights reserved. This book or any portion thereof may not be reproduced or used in any manner whatsoever without the express written permission of the publisher except for the use of brief quotations in a book review.

Printed in the United States of America

First Printing

978-1-943284-73-3 (pbk)

978-1-943284-76-4 (ebk)

A2Z Books Publishing Lithonia, GA 30058 www.A2ZBooksPublishing.net Manufactured in the United States of America A2Z Books Publishing has allowed this work to remain exactly as the author intended, verbatim.

A Letter to my Sons

To my sons the back bones of my life. You've inspired me to build the empire that we've built! You may be tried physically, tested mentally and it may even take your last breathe, but remember I will be with you always and forever. I know I'm a woman and I cannot raise you to be men, but I'll give it all I have until I have nothing left. If time was infinity I wouldn't apply as much pressure, but since we knows time is limited, always remember your mom said if the world shakes, your crown will never tilt.

Myn'less Koncepts

Your desire to change must be greater than your desire to stay the same

-Unknown

As the rainfall, I see the innocence and their tears.

As the lightning cracks like the whip, I feel that enhanced its imprint in my fears. As the thunder roars to hide my muffle as the rain runs down my back and rinses the blood from the scars into this puddle

Adding to the soil of the grass of the land that's now thick and green from my DNA you'd think my blood was cow manure

Could've fooled me after all the bullshit my people had to endure

It's amazing how a puddle something so big starts from a raindrop something so small it's easier to cry as the rainfall.

– Mynless

CONTENTS

The Outline of my Oppression

"Silenced"...1

"Black Crows and their Little white Lie's"............................3

Fear is Panic, Panic is Fear!...5

My Opinion of the blueprint..6

Folk tale of talking turtle...9

"Negus"..10

Desegregate the segregated!...12

He said, she said, they said!...13

"Mosey On down Jim Crow"...15

"Jim Crow Shadows."...17

"My 40 acres and a Mule"..18

"Majority of the Minorities"...20

"The Conscious of a clear mind."...21

Araminta...24

"The Pain of Art."..26

"The Jungle of a Panther"..27

"Oppressing my Oppressor" 29

"Rebelling against my Rebellion" 30

"Forbidden" 32

"Freedom" 34

"Bittersweet" 35

Momma Tell me 36

"Justice" 39

"My Brother's Keeper my Sister's Protector" 41

" Your Word is Bondage" 42

"The Question Game" 43

"Melanin" 46

"Imitation of my history" 48

"The Labeling of My Tattoo" 49

"Live by the Code" 51

"The Contradiction of the Innocence" 53

Double Entendre 55

" Detoxin my Toxin" 56

Last of a Dying breed 57

"Broken English" 59

viii

I didn't raise you to be silent
– Afeni Shakur

"SILENCED"

I will not be silenced by, the voices of the speechless.

I will not be hidden by the blind.

I will not be betrayed by the wicked

I will not be counted out by the countless of a misconstrued numeric system.

I will not be weakened by the powerless.

I will not be suffocated by the breathless.

I will not be moved by the motionless

My innocence will no longer bleed guilty by the victim.

MYN'LESS KONCEPT

I rather die on my feet, then live on my knees

– Huey Newton

"BLACK CROWS AND THEIR LITTLE WHITE LIE'S"

Black Crow, I'm glad that you soar so freely, be careful cause other birds don't like when you fly too high.

Black Crow, be careful where you land; all smiling faces don't mean your welcomed.

Black Crow, before you take off to your future, fly back to your past visit.

Alabama 1931 Scottsboro boys: Charlie Weems, Eugene Williams, Willie Roberson, Olen Montgomery, Clarence Norris, Ozzie Powell, Andrew wright, and young Roy wright 12 or 13 years of age. Haywood Patterson They all may be underage of 20. They all will be sentenced to death row all, but Roy Wright tells him he will be sentenced to life in prison. They will Be tried four times: Ollie, Willie, Roy, and Eugene will be freed after six years in jail.12 years later, Charlie, Andrew Clarence, and Ozzie were released on Parole. Remind Haywood, who was the one that was most hated, so he would have to escape in 1948, he will be free. The state of Alabama will declare their pardons on November 21, 2013.

Fly to South Carolina 1944 visit George Stinnely Jr. tell him that his trial will only last two hours the jury will only take 10 minutes to convict him

The 4 boys in Groveland, Florida -1949 tell them that Samuel Shepard is shot in the forehead dies instantly. While Walter Irving gets shot in the neck and chest but live to tell the story…then get convicted for a murder he didn't' commit. Charley Greenly, who was homeless. Ernest Greenly didn't make it out the woods.

Speaking of woods, if you don't believe me fly over Rosewood January 1st, 1923.

See black crow a lot of other black crows soared, suffered from a little white Lie.

FEAR IS PANIC, PANIC IS FEAR!

Fear is Panic, Panic is fear.

I feared that he would hit me, so I panicked and struck him out of fear

He became too powerful, so I panicked, and I silenced him out of fear.

Fear is panic, Panic is fear.

I'll depend on him to raise his voice to gain control of the home, but if he gains to much control then

I'll have to silence him. If he speaks against me, then I will have to make him flea like I did

Eledger, or assonate him Like I did Hammond

Fear is Panic, Panic is fear.

If he shows no fear, then I'll panic like I did and assonate him like I did Malcom.

I fear that the Minorites will ban together and rise above and I will panic and frame them like I did Angela Davis

Fear is panic, Panic is fear

I fear that I will no longer be called America, I panic that they will stand together

Fear is Panic, Panic is fear.

MY OPINION OF THE BLUEPRINT

My opinion of the blueprint is that we, the minorities, are subject to fail. Let's see what America taught me in my history of my ancestors is that to make it in life, you must gain control. To gain control, you must first weed out the strong, leaving the weak to become a liability. The weak will then rely on others to gain the confidence to gain strength, to gain security. When the weak are in fear. I'll then gain control. Don't believe me, think back to slavery when the male role model in a family was taking out of the home, children had to depend on momma, momma while working day in and day out, struggling turned to a structured religion. Still can't see the picture well fast forward to today's generation. Some fathers are nowhere in the family picture leaving the children to depend on the mother to take care of him. The women are the main ones working to provide… only in the black community.

It's just my opinion of the blueprint.

In my American history, minorities where the dominant ones; their mind's where so creative that I America was built on their blood sweat and tears. They can build a house ground up; they work hard and could concur the world if given the opportunity. So how can I control this because I don't like how it has my people looking weak. SO, what way can I make the minorities dependent. Think, think. I know I'll start depression and It will be great. Maybe if I enhance the business of pawnshops continue this thing call debt since the people are trying to ban peonage. The Minorities will lose everything, and once again, I'll gain control. America you smart, I'll start this thing called Welfare for my people, so they can survive.

It's just my opinion of the blueprint.

Damn, the minorities once again found a way to make things work, so let me build this thing called a ghetto. In these projects, we place the minorities, and we put a cap on their ability to survive, they can't make this much so their rent must be this much. They can't work this many hours, they must do enough just to get by but report everything they have. While we are at it add food stamps and welfare checks to the list, we need to gain control. In order to do that we must control their livelihood

It's just my opinion of the blueprint.

MYN'LESS KONCEPT

He learned wisdom and discretion and how to keep silent when it was necessary.

– Randolph Vance, Herbert Halpart, Glen Rounds

FOLK TALE OF TALKING TURTLE.

One day the towns motor mouth was walking down the street, and he was once again telling everybody's business. Telling everybody how he was about to do this, how he was about to accomplish that. One day he walked upon a turtle, and he began to speak to the turtle stating, "hey Mr. turtle today is going to be a great day, yes, it is.' The turtle raised his head and replied. "you talk too much.' The man standing in disbelief and asked, what did you say? The turtle replied, you talk too much, talking to much is going to cost you your life." The man ran over town, telling people about this talking turtle. Then he stopped one man saying, 'Hey, man, you won't believe this, I found a turtle that could talk." The man said, "Man, you know a turtle can't talk." Then the town motor mouth said man if this turtle doesn't talk, you can kill me. So, the men went searching for the turtle. Once they got to the turtle, the towns motor mouth said. "Mr. turtle, please show this man you can talk." The turtle just sat there. The man looked at the towns motor mouth. As the town's motor mouthed kept begging the turtle to talk. Finally, the towns motor mouth looked at the man and said, "this may not be the turtle." The man looked at him, pulled out his gun, and said, "Now, you said if he doesn't talk, then I can shoot you dead." The man aimed his gun and fired. The turtle then eased his way to the towns motor mouth, and before he took his last breath, the turtle said, "See, I told you, you talk too much."

"NEGUS"

My King, let me love you. My King let me go to God with you, so we can pray you through whatever you are about to face when you walk out this door. My King allow me to respect you as the man you are and the provider your about to become. My King allow me to genuinely feed your Spirit while I nourish your soul. Allow me to give you some of my strength I must cover you when you feel weak. My King allow me to pick you up when you fall, allow me to be that shoulder when you need to cry. My King allow me to be that hand to help you up. My king allow me to love you, my king allow me to be in love with you. My king allow me to fall to my knees and Pray for you and pray for us.

My King allow me to build you up, My King allow me to encourage you.

My king allow me to inspire you, my king allow me to motivate you. My king allow me to be your spine when your back has been broken by the oppress. My King, I do not uplift you so strong out of fear of you leaving me for another women. My king, I uplift you so much and love you so strong because I know you walk into a world that claims to be color blind but still live in black and white.

My King, you are a King!

The secret to life is to have no fear: it's the only way to function.
– Stokely Carmichael

DESEGREGATE THE SEGREGATED!

Familiar with the phrase United we stand Divided, we fall?

How can we stand together when we as a community is segregated?

We must first desegregate the segregated.

Black on Black crime was installed in the black community

Why because once again I needed the control,

Drugs was introduced to the community because once again I needed control

We must first desegregate the segregated

Tell them that the laws of the land are Money, power, respect

Trick them into believing that they need those three things and watch them kill to get it that will segregate the minorities

If you see one trying to stand out and go against my blueprint, we must assassinate them lets gain control by installing fear into the minds of the weak.

We must first desegregate the segregated.

Tear the community apart make them hate each other

Confuse their history make them think that if it wasn't for me, then they wouldn't be where they are, and they wouldn't be who they are.

My people

We must first desegregate the segregation

HE SAID, SHE SAID, THEY SAID!

Dr. Martin Luther King said, "he refused to accept the view mankind had tragically bound to the starless midnight of racism and war the bright daybreak of peace and brotherhood can never become a reality.

Dr. Mae Jemison said, "never be limited by other people's limited imaginations."

Audre Lorde Said, 'It's not our differences that divide us. It is our inability to recognize, accept, and celebrate those differences.

He said, she said, they said.

W.E.B. Du Bois said, "The cost of liberty is less than the price of repression."

Coretta Scott king said, Hate is too great a burden to bear. It injures the hater more than it injures the hated."

Thurgood Marshall said, in recognizing the humanity of our fellow beings, we pay ourselves the highest tribute."

He said, she said, they said!

Carol Mosley – Braun said, "Defining myself, as opposed to being defined by others, is one of the most difficult challenges I face."

Franklin Thomas said, "One day our decedents will think it incredible that we paid so much attention to things like the amount of melanin in our skin or the shape of our eyes or our gender instead of the unique identities of each of us as complex human beings."

Fredrick Douglas said,' "if there is no struggle,
then there is no progress."

Colin Powell said, "Have a vision. Be demanding."

Phillip Randolph said, "Freedom is never given it's won.

Kayne West said. "Black don't need a month;
we make history every day.

He said, she said, they said.

"MOSEY ON DOWN JIM CROW"

One day a stranger came into town singing,

From 1829 all the way to my dying day's I will still live on past my grave.

My folk will suffer in my shadow

Mosey on down Jim crow.

Folk would look at me as if I'm crazy,

But they will enslave your mind that's why it's for me

To segregate you from every other race

Times going to get dark, darker than my face.

From 1829 all the way to my dying day's I will still live on past my grave.

My folk will suffer in my shadow

Mosey on down Jim Crow.

Whites are superior to Blacks in all ways.

Whites and blacks' breeding would produce a mongrel race

Violence is acceptable to keep blacks in check

A black man couldn't shake the hand of a white man.

MYN'LESS KONCEPT

From 1829 all the way to my dying day's I will still live
on past my grave

My folk will suffer in my shadow

Mosey on down Jim crow.

"JIM CROW SHADOWS."

As Jim Crow went from town to town all through the south Setting different laws for each state that applied to all southern states He left a separation that divided a nation.

Any group standing for equality, either it be Black panthers, Muslims, or a man who believes in equality, is considered a terrorist.

The KKK believes in separation and that / he's superior.

A minority can walk down the street with his hands to his side, and be gun down by officers

A white man can murder 13 people and get treated to burger king.

Violence is still taking place by the superior to keep the minorities inline.

Separation is simple and clear; you can see it by looking at neighborhoods… majority of whites live and gated communities… majority of the blacks live across the tracks.

Can you think of other ways that play a part in Jim Crow shadows?

"MY 40 ACRES AND A MULE"

The Plot: Homestead act of 1862, any adult that is; born or will become a citizen and never raised arms against America will be granted 160 acres of surveyed government land.

The contradiction: 1857, the court ruled that negroes free or slaved were not citizens.

So, you mean to tell me that my ancestors blood sweat and tears have been poured on land that they may never get to own? You mean to tell me, that alone don't qualify me for an Acre?

So, the pain and suffrage of my ancestors do not qualify me for the foundation to build my children and me... No, so I must sit back and live in a community that you America built to fight for survival. Work twice as hard for better education, a better life.

No, give me what you owe me, I want my 40 acres and my mule.

The cost of living goes up yearly, but my pay remains the minimum wage. You think you make me feel special because my raise is now minimum wage?

You won't me to rely and depend on a government who hates me?... Better yet depend on a system that's set up for me to fail.

No, give me what you owe me, I want my 40 acres and a mule.

Now my 40 acres and a mule doesn't necessarily mean land and a car. Allow me to be able to get the best knowledge without overpricing my education. Allow me to build my business without putting stipulations on its foundation.

It's our land, and we want it now, you had minority folks thinking it was impossible, but not now Obama broke that barrier when we gained 50 states and a white house.

"MAJORITY OF THE MINORITIES"

How is it that the majority is one race that over rules the minority, which is made up of multiple races ?!? Who gave you the right to even place me in a category that I don't agree with or I don't fit into. How dare you say that minorities are anyone who is "non Hispanic white." Last time I checked African Americans where isolated in their own category, my skin has been frowned upon by the Jews, the Asians even Hispanics. When in reality melanin dominates all

If the definition of majority is - greater part, more than half of the total, and the majority rule mean the greater number should exercise greater power…Is that not an act of Jim crow Laws "all whites rain superior over non whites. Is that not a contradiction of your understanding. So, is calling whites the majority is that not saying whites reign superior over all races'… well there you have it I guess Majorities do rule Minorites

"THE CONSCIOUS OF A CLEAR MIND."

For me to gain power and control, let me install fear… How can I install fear into a powerful community?

Let's figure out how we can make the independent, become dependent. We must first install fear in the community. Allow them to panic and fear to the point where they must rely on the media for Clearitiy. We do this, we will have a system that will work until the end of time. Years ago, slave masters took the strongest man whom they called the man dingo warrior. The male was the dominant one… head of the household. The family looked at the male as the supporter and the female as the nurture. Take the male from the house and either sale him or burn him in front of the whole community that will install fear and the ones who remain take the slave master and let him rape the male in front of his family that will break his Spirit. Once the male is out of the picture, it will cause confusion. The children will rely on the mother, the mother would have to provide. Eventually, the race will be so use to the male leaving it will become natural. The woman being the only provider, the child will grow up and eventually depend on a woman to take care of them. The race will depend on the woman who is now the nurture and provider. Eventually, the mother will need to provide for her children so we will raise the cost of living and keep the pay at minimum wage, making the mother dependent on working two jobs, but if the mother works two jobs, then she won't be able to be in the home, leaving the children to raise themselves. Which they would have to learn how to maintain and provide for themselves even if it means stealing to make their own money; either way, they will end up in the system.

MIND OF THE SPEECHLESS

"I've freed thousands of slaves, would have freed more if they only knew they were slaves

– Harriet Tubman

ARAMINTA

I am standing in a field looking in the night sky

I see a woman in torn clothes run pass me, she stopped and said, "run,"

I look into the direction from which she came, I see lights looking like fire flies coming from the woods. I took off I didn't believe my eyes until I heard the sounds of coonhounds barking.

Ironically, I fall, I noticed this hole in the bottom of the bark of this big ole oak tree. I hide inside a man's hand, grabbed me by the mouth, and asked me not to scream. I turn, and through the moonlight, I can make out his face. It's Mr. Nate Turner he says, " the truth will always lie in the unconscious mind." Your unconscious is more real than your consciousness! I heard singing. I turned to find a field of slaves. I see the woman again, she's singing. I look back at Mr. Nate, he says, she's about to free some slaves. The humming got louder

I suddenly woke up to me singing.

I urge people to take the extra step of knowledge and learn about culture. I feel uncomfortable unless I learn. I'm going to take the time and effort to learn it.

— Zendaya

"THE PAIN OF ART."

I am a work of art, inside out.

From the melanin that coats my skin

To the genetics that molded and sculpted my figure.

To the lashes that formed my stretch marks

From the history of my ancestors to the cells of humiliation that

Forms my tough skin.

From the roots of my hair that twist into a map that locks into my freedom

From the homage paid to my genuine well being

All the way to the mockery of my very

Existence.

Don't just purchase my culture. Pay the price to live it.

"THE JUNGLE OF A PANTHER"

Notice how the jungle is filled with trees and different animals like a

World full of destruction

Yet the panther's stride with pride with its every step

How its stare alone can cause

One to pause dead in its tracks.

How he strides in with a pose so, dominate

That even a Jaguar tense up.

How he moves in silence to concur and dominates its pray.

How he can climb the tallest tree

His world has to offer,

Still, his credibility is limited

…could it be his melanistic silk coat.

MYN'LESS KONCEPT

Oppression: Noun

Prolonged cruel or unjust treatment or control

"OPPRESSING MY OPPRESSOR"

I stand against every lie you've ever tried to make me lie down for

Every story that your journalist tried to cover.

I've payed my suffrages of every

Debt you've created

I've taken every hindrance

You gave me

I've portrayed every misstate that

You claimed me to be.

My persona rebelled against your conformist government

My skin alone pressured my oppressor

"REBELLING AGAINST MY REBELLION"

How am I supposed to change a stubborn mind that was taught from the start that it was a slave?

How can I tell you to stop pledging to a flag that its very existence alone don't stand for you? How can I convince you that it's not ignorance, but the education they fear?

How can I convince you to go against the very culture you w ere forced to?

Create

how can I ask you to change your mind that your ways are as ignorant as those who oppress you?

The hate you create for your own kind is because of the lack of self-love.

How can I tell you that you have to strip your old ways?

And change your train of thought

Would my fight be worthless?

You'll never know until you

rebel against your rebellion

I can still taste the sin of you on my lips

– Nikki Andrews

"FORBIDDEN"

This morning when I opened my eyes, I then realized

That we had to part our ways and say our goodbyes

I no longer react when one calls your name, I cannot speak for others to whom you

Caused pain.

I know your diverse, but you've become part of my culture

After years of you haunting my existence like a vulture.

You could never bring one a happily ever after

Your name alone can defame one's character

Everything I stand for and using you is so contradictive, better yet its forbidden.

Why I keep reverting to you, I keep asking

I should have let you go July 7th when they threw

Dirt on your casket

To colonize one's mind, you must first demonize their culture than their traditions

– Unknown

"FREEDOM"

Look at him standing so firm and bold

While his eyes have me frozen as his voice serenates my soul

I place my hands where his chest is as my lips part from his… leaving me breathless

I want you to continue to insert in me yourself worthy

To where I no longer feel worthless insert in me so deep

Til I climax my purpose.

My how the tables turn from his eyes I see his damaged heart turned cold

entrust your heart with me I would love you from my soul, but his cold eyes made me come to the conclusion

that he doesn't notice me, so I walked away from his picture and woke up from my illusion.

He promised me this, in reality, he will no longer cause pain. He's done with the mind games

Although I can't see them, I still feel the chains

"BITTERSWEET"

I am more than my body, but yet the world insists on fucking me

Growing up there was never enough money rumors my mother was a whore my father is a junkie

Now they are sitting back watching they baby girl getting molested by the economy

Every day I strive and grind my teeth trying to get this taste out of my mouth

Oh, so bittersweet!

I have come to the conclusion that the system is created for blacks to sale their souls

Through drugs or prostitution or is it just an illusion every day I grind my teeth trying to get this taste out my mouth

Oh, so bittersweet!

MOMMA TELL ME

Momma, please tell me why do you teach me to love all, and all do not love me?

Momma why in order for me to be successful I have

To work ten times harder than others.

Momma, why is black history month one of the shortest months of the year.

How come the media only shine the light on my people for crimes but dim the light on the up and coming inventors

Momma why do they only teach me about the ones who have been assassinated

Momma how is it possible that innocent people are incarcerated, but yet

Criminals are walking around free.

Momma, why is it that one can commit murder get probation if not a few years, but if the police stop me, I get killed.

Why should I be subjected to inequality?

Momma, why haven't you taught me about racism.

Momma why am I taught that all we were; were

Slaves.

MIND OF THE SPEECHLESS

Why does my history tell me that the Klan's men where police, and politics?

Momma why do I feel like my truth is vanishing

Momma, why haven't you taught me that the dangerous place for a black man is a white man's imagination.

Momma, why do you keep telling me,

" a Black man have no win."

Justice: Noun

Just behavior, fairness…a concern for justice peace and genuine respect for people.

"JUSTICE"

I thought the goal was to protect and serve.

I thought that innocents where innocent until proven guilty.

I thought that once facts prove my innocents, then I'm no longer guilty

How do I go from a bullshit ass stop to

Fitting a description.

How did I go from Kings to slaves.

From victims to criminals

How is it that an innocent man life is taking for selling CDs on a corner to being choked to death by the hands of those who's suppose to protect and

Serve. No, I'm not talking about Spike Lee's "Do the Right thing."

How is it that a single mother serves time and gets her children taken away for trying to go to a job interview and leaves two months and a 6 year old in a car. to better her life for her and her children . while another got high and drove miles with her two month old on top of the car and the baby fell off the car she only gets probation

A woman fire a gun as a warning to her attacker gets 20 years

While another shoots an escort for not having sex with him and is acquitted for murder.

MYN'LESS KONCEPT

One gets 51 years for killing a man she was sold to in sex trafficking

While one gets 6 months for raping an unconscious woman.

One is shot 20 times behind a cell phone while another is rewarded after killing 9 people and armed.

I guess a mattress is not the only thing that wears a sheet

Don't worry Mr. officer when you say protect and serve

Your actions show "JUST US!"

"MY BROTHER'S KEEPER MY SISTER'S PROTECTOR"

I wouldn't ever put you in the position where you have to choose between your life or your freedom

your beauty will be uplifted by me.

my love, there's a tough road ahead of you

I'll pray the strength to ease your peace.

I'm here to encourage your security

For every insecurity, you've ever had.

I will not judge you for your past I'll support your present

So you can concur with your future.

I will not continue to allow hate to keep us divided

I've seen the strength of love when we bind together

I am my brother's keeper and my sister's protector.

"YOUR WORD IS BONDAGE"

You've created the rules and regulations of these laws and stipulations.

Where although you claim slavery no longer exists,

But I cannot believe you cause yet we are owned by a government

Whom controls where we live and how much we can work for. No! Well, excuse me if I got my definition of slavery confused. Please explain to me just promise that your word wouldn't have me bound in bondage.

How you created this egalitarianism, but yet I'm still bound to inequality.

You have emancipation, but yet you tighten the reins on the bridle of my people's freedom this just my opinion; just promise me your word wouldn't have me bound in bondage.

You overwork, but underpay me your protected by labor laws

Your business loans make it hard for me to work for myself… yet I have to enslave myself to make another rich. You say it's work my thoughts say its chattel slavery. Promise me your word wouldn't have me bound in bondage… Never mind history repeats its self as we all can see. My history proves that your word will always bond me to bondage.

"THE QUESTION GAME"

Why is that in every city with an urban area have street names such as; Martin Luther King, Malcom X, and are across the tracks, but Almost every school in the urban areas are Named after generals?

Why is it when your sons do something, "their just, boys being boys, but when my sons walk down the street their considered dangerous. Could it be that the melanin in their skin is a powerful weapon. Is it that my sons Presence alone makes your chakra kneel. Why is there so much hatred in your heart is it that you can see the warrior in my eyes. Or feel the power from my soul. Why is it that majority claims to be superior, but go out their way to dominate the minority. Why is it that one group who wants equality, love, and prosperity looked at as terrorist, but the main ones causing terrorist acts is crowned; Politicians, lawyers, DA. Judges, polices. Why is it that; that your history teaches me that I'm nothing more than a lying thief and common prostitute. When my history shows me that I come from a land of riches where one would kill to inherit my bloodline. Why is it that one child can be taught to by a veteran how to shoot a pistol at the age of six and another gets charged with child endangerment for holding their child with a gun in the back ground. Why is it one can wear a confederate flag freely, but as soon as I push a fist in there, which states peace and unity for all, I'm considered racist. Why is black history only 28 days? Well, I guess if it takes you 30 days to learn about the two you've assassinated, I couldn't imagine the time it takes to teach about the survivors.

"My Melanin is powerful.

It threatens the ignorant, challenges the misinformed. My articulation intimidates. It demands respect the moment I speak."

– Nii Lee Cyrus

"MELANIN"

Its feet stand tall and firm as which the land my ancestors come from

The melanin in my body is as rich as its soil.

Natural and pure as its oil

It protects my Charisma with every stitch my genetics sow

from when the sun hit and enhance my natural glow,

that's why my age is a mystery it's like the reason I never look old

its as solid, but yet worth more than gold.

its essence cannot be sold

It makes hate gag as if it's being throttled.

Your lack of imitation couldn't even hold it

In a bottle

You can mimic a result,

But not creativity.

– Sonya Teclai

"IMITATION OF MY HISTORY"

They lied police brutality never died

All my rights have been wronged my innocence have been labeled guilty

My equality is still unequal.

How did I go from the top of a pyramid to the bottom of a food-chain.

How is it that I'm judged not by the purity of

My love, but off yourself hate

In slavery, they made examples out of slaves by torcher and killing

Them in front of other slaves to install fear

Some male slave masters

Would rape the male slaves in front of his family

To break his Spirit don't think that it's from

History do your research ill make it easy to watch penitentiary.

"THE LABELING OF MY TATTOO"

Once again, my innocents doesn't mean anything. Seems like my mother should of named me guilty the day she Gave birth to me. I have had soldiers who stood on the frontline

So I can even walk on the same sidewalk. Still this day, I'm asked, "where I'm headed?' then it goes from where you headed to me fitting a description. Good thing I'm not my brothers because maybe they'd try to throw a couple of punches. I' was told that I am given the same opportunity as others, but on every application I fill out, it asks my race.

I mean there's no box to mark human.

Let me not get started on my private education schools all the way to college is for well off citizens. I'm grateful for financial aid, but don't think I that you are doing me a favor. Shouldn't it be free every other culture except us got their reparation. Speaking of school

What scientists dropped out of college before they finished the projects

My people still walking around, looking like rats scratching for survival.

That was rhetorical. I answered that in the question game that's in the past pages. One page after "your word is bondage," but twenty pages after my opinion of a blueprint. Excuse me if I have more questions that cause me to be judge by the melanin that creates the art that makes up my ink in my permeant tattoo.

"LIVE BY THE CODE"

What is civil rights, who's to say what they are?

My civil rights say I have the right to vote. You may have taken out the "literacy test," and replace it with stipulations such as "felons don't have a right to vote," but minorities are felons the moment they are born. The only way around that is if one is bribed or if one is pardon your OG was trying to teach you Because he knew we're not the only ones living by code

I have the right to a fair trial. Its where ones rights are safeguarded until he's proven guilty, But evidence proves my innocence. I still have to serve time as if I was guilty. I have to be incarcerated until my trail others can be on house arrest.

Your OG was trying to teach you because he knew we're not the only ones living by code.

I have the right to government assistance that the government once again put its limits on. I can work 40 hours a week, even over time. No matter how much in taxes, don't worry, I still wouldn't be qualified because I cannot make a certain amount before taxes is taken out. It's one of those situations your "damned if you do, damned if you don't." either way you're going to struggle

MYN'LESS KONCEPT

Your OG was trying to teach you because he knew we're not the only ones living by code.

The right to public education should I translate that for you. We'll allow you to have and education to where you can read and write well enough to work for someone else. What's so different about private school besides the fact that its another way to keep school segregation, I guess, that's a barrier that the up and coming Ruby Bridges have to break.

Your OG was trying to teach you because he knew we're not the only ones living by the code

I'm allowed to walk into public facilities, but I would be followed as if I don't work hard like the next.

Your OG knew your civil rights would be contradicted by a black code

"THE CONTRADICTION OF THE INNOCENCE"

I'm trying to find the balance and stress the importance to my children to Love others, while their treading that fine line of hate.

When is the appropriate time for me to teach my sons that they can be as free as their mind take them, but they live in a world that would bridle them with stipulations of the uncertainty of what's innocent and what's not.

How can I teach you not to be racist, but I have to teach you about racism

How you can have fun with any race, but by the color of your skin

You will be singled out.

I can encourage them to be great in whatever their destined to become, but how can you bring yourself to tell your child that they are not equal

Do I raise my children as children where they can play laugh and have that same childhood we did where we didn't know the true meaning of struggling was because we were surrounded by our own. We played not knowing we were teaching ourselves how to survive.

Do I remain in the same situation because I feel that I can protect them better from the streets than the system.

Until death takes me and… then I will forever live in the of fear death taking me, then who's going to protect my babies.

In reality, I want better for them to show them that they are more than what society gives them, so I leave for the suburbs

So do I teach my children that they would have to work twice as hard,

and they have to be careful walking up and down the sidewalk because they would be labeled as targets.

How do I teach my children that they already destined for the penitentiary?

At the age of 7

Regardless of their innocence

Do I teach them that she don't have to speak English all she has to do is point? How do I tell them that the odds are against them?

It breaks my heart, looking at their smiling innocent faces knowing that one day I must tell them that they have to be subjected to oppression.

DOUBLE ENTENDRE

Isn't it amazing how the tree of life is symbolic of unity, which is deeply rooted in our mines?

Ironic how I'm swinging back and forward as my neck is gracefully throttled by its own vines.

Like its branches, we grow in different directions

As my body dangle from its branches that hold the rope that threads around my neck like a Japanese Wisteria while your bullets pierce my body leaving holes of fear

As my body burns from the hate of fire, you set to it.

You would think that the fire would spread and destroy the rest of the tree, but like my Spirit, it remains unblemished

That's the way I vision the tree of life.

" DETOXIN MY TOXIN"

I engulfed enough toxins in my body to

Posion a small towns water supply.

My mind has been programmed to the point where I see the media reprogramming the walls of my membrane

me fighting and trying to hold onto the truth makes the

joker looks sane.

I'm stuck between the levels of their hatred and my level of allowance

I inhale more herbal substance to maintain the balance.

I swallowed enough sweetness from the sugarcane of oppression

The protein from the vegetables of my body now rejects the strength of my aggression.

The rotten fruit of justice that soothes my rage

Has overthrown the purpose of my burning sage.

LAST OF A DYING BREED

Have you ever sat back and thought about how something is taken for granted. How certain people fight off poulters to save your life. Have the world fight for your life. Your very existence can be taken away by the stray bullet that's held by hate and fired by greed. Noticed how my children are still endangered to be victims or sold off to the highest bidder or their freedom is taken away, or how they may have to spend life behind bars. For the world to view you. Funny how the only time the endangered spices is portrayed as a dangerous beast is when it's locked in a caged controlled by man and watch as its history fades away. I know I cannot imagine the world without African American men

Accountability

Sometimes playing the victim is easier than having to look within ourselves and take accountability for how we got in the mess in the first place. Taking accountability is a way to take our power back.

– ashalvesblog.com

"BROKEN ENGLISH"

It's amazing how you have to use proper English on that nine to five just make ends meet. How you have to become someone else to survive and take the chance of not being accepted in the street of hard knocks. You've created this world of confusion where you've put yourself in a box.

Not only good enough for this "blue-collared," society, but your environment won't let you become more than your neighborhood prodigy.

Stuck between looking like an "Uncle tom" or a "snake" for hustler, either way, you can't be trusted. Better not try to make it; you will be pulled down by those crabs in the bucket. How can I argue that the world we live in inmates the mosquito in the jar irrigardeless of the culture immations it's you that's placing your own stipulations. There's a lack of intelligence, but a boost of ignorance keeps this up slavery will never be finished....

Forgive me for my broken english

Contact Myn'less Koncept @MynlessKoncept on Instagram

Interested in Writing/Publishing a book contact Dr. Synovia @www.a2zbookspublishing.net or @Dr.Synovia on Instagram.

www.ingramcontent.com/pod-product-compliance
Lightning Source LLC
Chambersburg PA
CBHW030137100526
44592CB00011B/925